If you were a

Synonym

by Michael Dahl
illustrated by Sara Gray

PICTURE WINDOW BOOKS
Minneapolis, Minnesota

Synonym (syn) a word that means the same thing, or almost the same thing, as another word

Editors: Christianne Jones and Dodie Marie Miller
Designer: Tracy Davies
Page Production: Lori Bye
Art Director: Nathan Gassman
The illustrations in this book were created with acrylics.

Picture Window Books
5115 Excelsior Boulevard
Suite 232
Minneapolis, MN 55416
877-845-8392
www.picturewindowbooks.com

Printed in the United States of America.

Library of Congress Cataloging-in-Publication Data
Dahl, Michael.
If you were a synonym / by Michael Dahl ; Illustrated by Sara Gray.
p. cm.—(Word fun)
Includes bibliographical references and index.
ISBN-13: 978-1-4048-2387-7 (library binding)
ISBN-10: 1-4048-2387-5 (library binding)
ISBN-13: 978-1-4048-2391-4 (paperback)
ISBN-10: 1-4048-2391-3 (paperback)
1. English language—Synonyms and antonyms—Juvenile literature. I. Gray, Sara, ill.
II. Title.
PE1591.D21 2006
428.1—dc22   2006027311

Special thanks to our advisers for their expertise:

Rosemary G. Palmer, Ph.D., Department of Literacy
College of Education, Boise State University

Susan Kesselring, M.A., Literacy Educator
Rosemount—Apple Valley—Eagan (Minnesota) School District

Looking for synonyms?

Watch for the big, colorful words in the example sentences.

If you were a synonym ...

...you could be
COOL, CHILLY, FROSTY, ICY, WINTRY, or FREEZING.

4

No matter how you say it, you would still be COLD.

Synonyms are words that mean the same thing, or almost the same thing, as another word.

HUGE is different than GIGANTIC ...

6

... but they both mean **BIG**!

If you were a synonym, you could change and still mean the same thing.

The thunder is **LOUD**,

BLASTING,

NOISY,

BOOMING,

DEAFENING, and

EAR-SPLITTING!

If you were a synonym, you wouldn't have to use the same word to describe the same activity.

The sled **PLUMMETED** down the hill and **ZIPPED** under the bridge.

The sled **PLUNGED** down the hill and **WHISKED** under the bridge.

If you were a synonym, you would keep sentences exciting and add variety.

The **DAZZLING,**
BRILLIANT,
LUMINOUS lightning
lit up the **DARK,**
HAZY night.

If you were a synonym, you could act as different parts of speech. You could be a noun. A noun is a word that names a person, place, or thing.

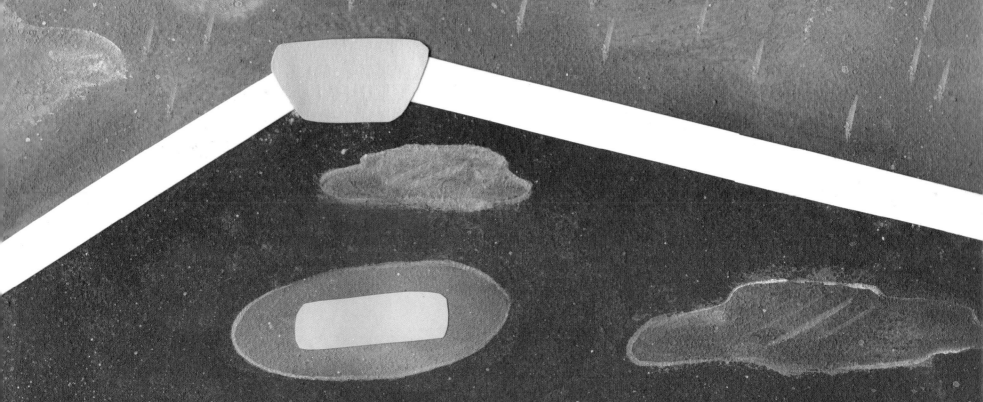

The game was canceled because of the **RAINSTORM,** the **RAIN SHOWER,** or the **DOWNPOUR.**

14

If you were a synonym, you could be a verb. A verb is used to express an action or condition.

The wind **SWEEPS,**

FLUTTERS, or SAILS over the land.

17

If you were a synonym, you could be an adjective. Adjectives describe or modify nouns or pronouns.

One **THIN, WISPY** cloud hung over

18

the **ARID, DRY** desert.

If you were a synonym, you would be found in a thesaurus. A thesaurus is a book full of synonyms and antonyms.

The temperature could be TOASTY, WARM, BOILING, BLISTERING, or TROPICAL.

No matter how you say it, the temperature is still **HOT**.

Fun with Synonyms

Have a group of friends split into two teams. It doesn't matter how many people are on each team. Next, have each group write a different word on 10 pieces of paper. Adjectives work best.

One team starts by drawing a piece of paper. They say the word out loud. For example, one team might draw "big." Then the other team must think of a synonym for "big." They might say "huge." The teams go back and forth, naming synonyms for "big," until one team is stumped. The team to think of the last synonym gets a point and gets to draw again.

The team with the most points after all of the words are drawn wins.

Fact: If you want to find a synonym, look in a thesaurus. You will see the abbreviation "syn" next to it. The "syn" stands for synonym.

23

Glossary

adjective—a word that describes or modifies a noun or pronoun

antonym—a word that has the opposite meaning of another word

modify—to change in some way

noun—a word that names a person, place, or thing

synonym—a word that means the same thing, or almost the same thing, as another word

thesaurus—a book full of synonyms and antonyms

verb—a word used to express an action or condition

To Learn More

At the Library

Cleary, Brian P. *Pitch and Throw, Grasp and Know: What Is a Synonym?* Minneapolis: Carolrhoda Books, 2005.

Heinrichs, Ann. *Synonyms and Antonyms.* Chanhassen, Minn.: Child's World, 2006.

On the Web

FactHound offers a safe, fun way to find Web sites related to this book. All of the sites on FactHound have been researched by our staff.

1. Visit www.facthound.com
2. Type in this special code: 1404823875
3. Click on the FETCH IT button.

Your trusty FactHound will fetch the best sites for you!

Index

Look for all of the books in the Word Fun series:

If You Were a Conjunction

If You Were a Homonym or a Homophone

If You Were a Noun

If You Were a Palindrome

If You Were a Preposition

If You Were a Pronoun

If You Were a Synonym

If You Were a Verb

If You Were an Adjective

If You Were an Adverb

If You Were an Antonym

If You Were an Interjection